THE MYSTIC LAND

A CULTURAL AND SPIRITUAL EXPLORATION OF INDIA

AF571261

DR. JAGADEESH PILLAI

Copyright © Dr. Jagadeesh Pillai
All Rights Reserved.

This book has been self-published with all reasonable efforts taken to make the material error-free by the author. No part of this book shall be used, reproduced in any manner whatsoever without written permission from the author, except in the case of brief quotations embodied in critical articles and reviews.

The Author of this book is solely responsible and liable for its content including but not limited to the views, representations, descriptions, statements, information, opinions and references ["Content"]. The Content of this book shall not constitute or be construed or deemed to reflect the opinion or expression of the Publisher or Editor. Neither the Publisher nor Editor endorse or approve the Content of this book or guarantee the reliability, accuracy or completeness of the Content published herein and do not make any representations or warranties of any kind, express or implied, including but not limited to the implied warranties of merchantability, fitness for a particular purpose. The Publisher and Editor shall not be liable whatsoever for any errors, omissions, whether such errors or omissions result from negligence, accident, or any other cause or claims for loss or damages of any kind, including without limitation, indirect or consequential loss or damage arising out of use, inability to use, or about the reliability, accuracy or sufficiency of the information contained in this book.

Made with ♥ on the Notion Press Platform
www.notionpress.com

|| Dedicated to all wisdom seekers around the World ||

ꕤ

Contents

Contents

PRAYER

"Om Bhadram Karnebhih Shrunuyaama DevaahBhadram Pashyemaakshabhiryajatraah Sthirairangaistushtuvaamsastanoobhih Vyashema Devahitam YadaayuhSwasti Na Indro VridhashravaahSwasti Nah Pooshaa VishwavedaahSwasti Nastaarkshyo ArishtanemihSwasti No Brihaspatir DadhaatuOm Shantih, Shantih, Shantih"

The literal meaning of this mantra is: OM. O Gods! Let us hear auspicious words from our ears. O reverent Gods! Let us behold propitious visions from our eyes, let our organs and body be stable, healthy, and strong. Let us do that which is pleasing to the gods in the life span allotted to us. May Indra, inscribed in the scriptures, bring us fortune! May Pushan, the knower of the world, grant us prosperity! May Trakshya, who vanquishes enemies, bestow us with blessings! May Brihaspati bring us success!
OM Peace, Peace, Peace.

About The Author

Dr. Jagadeesh Pillai is a renowned Guinness World Record holder, writer, and researcher hailing from Varanasi, also known as the abode of Lord Shiva. With a Ph.D. in Vedic Science and a range of creative ideas and achievements, he is a true polymath. He is the author of more than 100 books including Research Publications. Although his roots can be traced back to Kerala, the people of Varanasi hold him in high regard and affectionately consider him one of their own.

In 1998, Dr. Pillai was offered a job at Banaras Hindu University, but he left the position after only two months to pursue greater goals in life. He believed that in order to study Indian scriptures and engage in other creative endeavours, he needed to retire from the daily grind of working solely for money at a young age.

He started an export business from scratch, using the knowledge he had gained from a previous job in the industry. His intelligence and unique approach to business led to great success in a short period of time, earning him more in just a decade and a half than he would have in a lifetime working in a government job. Upon the passing of Dr. APJ Abdul Kalam, Dr. Pillai decided to leave the business and dedicate himself to reading, studying, researching, and experimenting.

During his tenure in the export business, Dr. Pillai traveled to over 16 countries, gaining valuable insight and experiencing the world and life in detail.

Dr. Pillai has achieved four Guinness World Records in the following subjects:

"Script to Screen" - In this record, Dr. Pillai produced and directed an animation film within the shortest time possible, breaking the previous record set by Canadians. He has also received numerous national and international awards and recognitions for this achievement.

Longest Line of Postcards - For this record, Dr. Pillai created a line of 16,300 postcards on the occasion of the 163rd anniversary of Indian Postal Day. The event also included a questionnaire about the Indian flag.

Largest Poster Awareness Campaign - Dr. Pillai designed an awareness campaign on the subject of "Beti Bachao - Beti Padhao" (Save the Girl Child - Educate the Girl Child) to achieve this record.

Largest Envelope - In tribute to the Indian Prime Minister's "Make in India" initiative, Dr. Pillai created a 4000 square meter envelope using waste paper to achieve this record.

Attempted - **70000 Candles on a 210 kg Cake** - To celebrate the 70th Indian Independence Day, Dr. Pillai attempted to light 70,000 candles on a 210 kg cake, which was recorded in World Records India.

Attempted - **Documentary on Dhamek Stupa of Sarnath in 17 Languages** - Dr. Pillai attempted to create a documentary on the Dhamek Stupa of Sarnath, dubbing it in 17 different languages. The result of this attempt is currently awaiting confirmation from the Guinness World Records.

Dr. Pillai is skilled in teaching the Bhagavad Gita, a Hindu scripture, and is popular among young people. He has helped many young people improve their lives through his motivational teachings.

In addition to teaching, he has composed and sung numerous Sanskrit Bhajans and patriotic songs.

He has also written and directed several short films and documentaries for awareness campaigns, and has volunteered with the police in both UP and Kerala to spread awareness about various issues through videos and photography.

Incredibly, he has produced and directed over 100 documentaries about the city of Varanasi, all on his own.

He has also helped and guided more than 25 boys and girls to achieve world records through creative and innovative methods. He is a multifaceted person who uses his intellect and the blessings given to him by God to excel in various areas. He is both a teacher and a student, always learning and teaching, and is able to master any subject he comes across.

He is a selfless social activist and motivational speaker who has overcome struggles and failures to become a successful and enthusiastic individual with a rich life experience.

In addition to his work with the Bhagavad Gita, he is also an efficient Tarot card reader, Astro-Vastu consultant, and a talented singer and composer. He has sung the entire Ram Charita Manas and Bhagavad Gita in his own compositions, and has sung the phrase "Lokah Samastha Sukhino Bhavantu" in 50 different languages. He is currently working on a detailed and scientific study of Vedas, Upanishads, Puranas, and the Bhagavad Gita. He has also composed and sung the Hanuman Chalisa and Gayatri Mantra in 108 and 1008 different compositions, respectively.

Awards - Four Times Guinness World Records, Winner of Mahatma Gandhi Vishwa Shanti Puraskar, Mahatma Gandhi Global Peace Ambassador, Kashi Ratna Award, Dr. APJ Abdul Kalam Motivational Person of the Year 2017, Mother Teresa Award, Indira Gandhi Priyadarshini Award, Bharat Vikas Ratna Award, Udyog Ratna Award, Vigyan Prasar Award, Poorvanchal Ratn Samman.

Preface

In the pages of "The Mystic Land: A Cultural and Spiritual Exploration of India," readers will embark on a captivating journey through the vibrant culture and spiritual traditions of India. From the bustling cities to the remote villages, this book offers an in-depth exploration of the country's unique customs, beliefs, and practices.

From the ancient Vedic scriptures to the modern-day spiritual movements, readers will gain a deeper understanding of India's spiritual heritage. They will learn about the various Hindu gods and goddesses, the importance of meditation and yoga, and the significance of the caste system. Additionally, readers will gain insight into the country's diverse cultural practices, such as its colorful festivals, its traditional music and dance, and its rich culinary traditions.

This book is an invitation to explore the many facets of India's culture and spirituality. It is a chance to discover the beauty and complexity of this ancient land, and to gain a deeper appreciation for its unique customs and beliefs. Through its vivid descriptions and engaging stories, readers will gain a greater understanding of India's spiritual and cultural landscape.

So come, join us on this journey of discovery. Let us explore the mystic land of India, and uncover its secrets and wonders.

I

The Sacred Geography of India

India is a land of spiritual and cultural richness, and its sacred geography is a testament to this. From the majestic Himalayas to the lush forests of the Western Ghats, India is home to some of the most sacred sites in the world. From the ancient temples of the south to the holy rivers of the north, these sites have been revered for centuries and continue to draw pilgrims from all over the world.

The Himalayas are home to some of the most sacred sites in India, including the four holy abodes of the Hindu gods. These are Badrinath, Kedarnath, Gangotri, and Yamunotri. These sites are believed to be the source of all spiritual power and are visited by millions of pilgrims each year.

The Western Ghats are home to some of the most sacred sites in India, including the ancient temples of Mahabalipuram and Kanchipuram. These temples are believed to be the abode of the gods and are visited by millions of pilgrims each year.

The holy rivers of India are also considered to be sacred sites. The Ganges, Yamuna, and Saraswati rivers are believed to be the source of all life and are visited by millions of pilgrims each year.

The sacred sites of India are not limited to the Himalayas and the Western Ghats. The Ajanta and Ellora caves in Maharashtra are believed to be the abode of the gods and are visited by millions of pilgrims each year. The Golden Temple in Amritsar is one of the most sacred sites in India and is visited by millions of pilgrims each year.

The sacred geography of India is a testament to its profound spiritual and cultural heritage. From the awe-inspiring Himalayas to the verdant forests of the Western Ghats, India is home to some of the most sacred sites on the planet. From the ancient temples of the south to the venerated rivers of the north, these places of worship and pilgrimage have been revered for centuries, providing a spiritual connection to the divine for millions of people.

"India is the cradle of the human race, the birthplace of human speech, the mother of history, the grandmother of legend, and the great grand mother of tradition."

- Mark Twain

ꙮ

II

Exploring the Temples of South India

Exploring the Temples of South India is a journey through a land of ancient gods and goddesses, a place of spiritual and cultural significance. From the majestic temples of Tamil Nadu to the sacred shrines of Karnataka, South India is a place of awe-inspiring beauty and spiritual power.

The temples of South India are a testament to the region's rich cultural heritage. From the intricately carved sculptures of the Chola dynasty to the grandeur of the Vijayanagara Empire, these temples are a reminder of the region's long and vibrant history.

The temples of South India are also a place of spiritual significance. For centuries, pilgrims have come to these temples to seek blessings from the gods and goddesses.

From the ancient Shiva temples of Tamil Nadu to the sacred shrines of Karnataka, these temples are a place of worship and devotion.

The journey through South India's temples is a journey of discovery. From the grandeur of the Meenakshi Temple in Madurai to the serenity of the Tirupati Temple in Andhra Pradesh, each temple offers a unique experience. Visitors can explore the intricately carved sculptures, marvel at the grand architecture, and experience the spiritual power of these sacred sites.

The temples of South India are also a place of cultural exploration. From the vibrant festivals of Tamil Nadu to the colorful rituals of Karnataka, visitors can experience the unique culture of the region. From the traditional music and dance of the region to the vibrant art and craft, South India is a place of cultural richness.

Exploring the temples of South India is a journey of discovery and spiritual awakening. From the majestic temples of Tamil Nadu to the sacred shrines of Karnataka, visitors can experience the beauty and spiritual power of this ancient land. From the grandeur of the Meenakshi Temple in Madurai to the serenity of the Tirupati Temple in Andhra Pradesh, each temple offers a unique opportunity to explore the rich cultural heritage of South India. Whether it's the intricate carvings of the Brihadeeswarar Temple in Thanjavur or the captivating architecture of the Chennakesava Temple in Belur, visitors can immerse themselves in the beauty and spirituality of these ancient sites.

"India is the meeting point of the spiritual and the material."

- Mahatma Gandhi

ꕤ

III

The Himalayan Mysticism: The Role of the Mountains in Indian Spirituality

The Himalayas have long been a source of spiritual and cultural inspiration for the people of India. From the ancient Vedic texts to the modern-day spiritual practices, the mountains have played an integral role in Indian spirituality.

The Himalayas are home to some of the most sacred sites in India, including Mount Kailash, the abode of Lord Shiva, and the source of the four great rivers of India. The mountains are also home to many ancient monasteries and temples, which are still visited by pilgrims from all over the world.

The Himalayas have been a source of spiritual guidance and enlightenment for centuries. The ancient Vedic texts describe the mountains as a place of great power and spiritual energy. The mountains are seen as a gateway to the divine, and many spiritual seekers have journeyed to the Himalayas in search of enlightenment.

The Himalayas are also home to many spiritual practices, such as yoga, meditation, and tantra. These practices are believed to help one connect with the divine and achieve spiritual growth. The mountains are also home to many spiritual teachers, who offer guidance and wisdom to those seeking spiritual enlightenment.

The Himalayas are also a source of great beauty and awe. The majestic peaks, lush valleys, and pristine lakes provide a breathtaking backdrop for spiritual exploration. The mountains are also home to many rare and endangered species, making them a haven for wildlife and nature lovers alike.

The Himalayas have long been a source of spiritual and cultural inspiration for the people of India, from the ancient Vedic texts to modern-day spiritual practices. These majestic peaks and lush valleys are a gateway to the divine, a source of spiritual guidance and enlightenment, and a haven for wildlife and nature lovers alike. The Himalayas are a place of great power and spiritual energy, offering a unique opportunity to explore the depths of one's soul and connect with the divine.

"India is a land of dreams and romance, of fabulous wealth and fabulous poverty, of splendor and rags, of palaces and hovels, of famine and pestilence, of genii and giants and Aladdin lamps, of tigers and elephants, the cobra and the jungle, the country of a thousand nations and a hundred tongues, of a thousand religions and two million gods, cradle of the human race, birthplace of human speech, mother of history, grandmother of legend, great-grandmother of tradition."

- Mark Twain

ꕤ

IV

The Sacred Rivers of India: A Cultural and Spiritual Exploration

India is a land of many sacred rivers, each of which has its own unique cultural and spiritual significance. From the Ganges in the north to the Godavari in the south, these rivers have been revered for centuries by Hindus, Buddhists, and Jains alike.

The Ganges is perhaps the most famous of India's sacred rivers. It is believed to be the most sacred river in Hinduism, and is often referred to as the "Mother Ganges". Hindus believe that bathing in the Ganges will purify their souls and bring them closer to the divine. The river is also a source of spiritual sustenance for Buddhists and Jains, who consider it to be a symbol of peace and tranquility.

The Yamuna is another important river in India, and is considered to be the sister of the Ganges. It is believed to be the source of all life, and is often referred to as the "Goddess Yamuna". Hindus believe that bathing in the Yamuna will bring them closer to the divine, and it is also a source of spiritual sustenance for Buddhists and Jains.

The Godavari is the third most sacred river in India, and is believed to be the source of all knowledge and wisdom. Hindus believe that bathing in the Godavari will bring them closer to the divine, and it is also a source of spiritual sustenance for Buddhists and Jains.

The Narmada is the fourth most sacred river in India, and is believed to be the source of all healing and rejuvenation. Hindus believe that bathing in the Narmada will bring them closer to the divine, and it is also a source of spiritual sustenance for Buddhists and Jains.

The Kaveri is the fifth most sacred river in India, revered as the source of all prosperity and abundance. Hindus believe that bathing in its waters will bring them closer to the divine, and that its waters are imbued with spiritual power. The Kaveri is a symbol of hope and renewal, and its waters are believed to bring good fortune and blessings to those who bathe in them.

"India is the land of a million gods and goddesses, and a billion people."

ᘓᘐ

V

Exploring the Cave Temples of India

India is a land of mysticism and spiritual exploration, and its cave temples are a testament to this. For centuries, these ancient structures have been a source of fascination for travelers and pilgrims alike. From the Ajanta and Ellora Caves in Maharashtra to the Badami Caves in Karnataka, these awe-inspiring monuments are a journey through time and space.

The Ajanta and Ellora Caves are some of the most famous cave temples in India. Located in the Aurangabad district of Maharashtra, these caves are a UNESCO World Heritage Site and are renowned for their intricate carvings and sculptures.

The Ajanta Caves are believed to have been built between the 2nd century BCE and 6th century CE, while the Ellora Caves were constructed between the 6th and 11th centuries.

These caves are a testament to the skill and artistry of the ancient Indian artisans, and their intricate carvings and sculptures depict scenes from Hindu, Buddhist, and Jain mythology.

The Badami Caves in Karnataka are another popular destination for spiritual exploration. These caves were built between the 6th and 8th centuries and are renowned for their intricate carvings and sculptures. The Badami Caves are home to some of the most beautiful and intricate sculptures in India, depicting scenes from Hindu, Buddhist, and Jain mythology.

Exploring the cave temples of India is a journey through time and space. From the Ajanta and Ellora Caves in Maharashtra to the Badami Caves in Karnataka, these awe-inspiring monuments are a testament to the skill and artistry of the ancient Indian artisans.

These caves are a source of fascination for travelers and pilgrims alike, and offer a unique insight into the spiritual and cultural heritage of India. From the intricate carvings and sculptures to the breathtaking views, these caves are a must-visit destination for anyone looking to explore the mystic land of India.

"India is the land of mystery and magic, of beauty and grace, of wisdom and knowledge."

ꕥ

VI

The Mystical City of Varanasi: A Cultural and Spiritual Exploration

Varanasi, also known as Benares or Kashi, is a city of immense spiritual and cultural significance in India. Located on the banks of the Ganges River, it is one of the oldest continuously inhabited cities in the world. It is a major pilgrimage site for Hindus, Buddhists, and Jains, and is considered to be one of the holiest cities in India.

The city of Varanasi is steeped in history and culture, and is a place of great spiritual significance. It is believed to be the place where the Hindu god Shiva first revealed himself to mankind, and is home to some of the most important Hindu temples in the country. The city is also home to many Buddhist and Jain temples, and is a major center of pilgrimage for followers of these religions.

The city of Varanasi is a vibrant and bustling place, with a unique atmosphere that is unlike any other city in India. The narrow streets are filled with people from all walks of life, and the air is filled with the smell of incense and the sound of chanting. The city is also home to a number of ancient monuments, including the famous ghats, or steps, that line the banks of the Ganges.

The spiritual and cultural significance of Varanasi is evident in its many temples, shrines, and monuments. The city is home to some of the most important Hindu temples in the country, including the Kashi Vishwanath Temple, the Sankat Mochan Temple, and the Durga Temple. The city is also home to many Buddhist and Jain temples, including the famous Sarnath Stupa, which is said to be the place where the Buddha first preached his teachings.

Varanasi is a renowned center of learning, boasting some of India's most prestigious universities, such as the Banaras Hindu University and the Sampurn. These universities are renowned for their academic excellence and have produced some of the country's most successful graduates. The city is also home to a variety of colleges and other educational institutions, providing a wealth of opportunities for students to pursue their studies. With its rich cultural heritage and vibrant academic atmosphere, Varanasi is an ideal destination for those seeking to further their education.

"India is the land of the eternal spirit, the land of the divine, the land of the infinite."

ꙮ

VII

The Land of the Siddhas: A Journey Through the Mystical South

The Land of the Siddhas: A Journey Through the Mystical South is a captivating exploration of India's spiritual and cultural heritage. From the ancient temples of Tamil Nadu to the sacred groves of Kerala, this journey takes readers on a captivating exploration of India's mystical south.

The Land of the Siddhas is a place of spiritual enlightenment, where the ancient sages and mystics of India have sought refuge for centuries. It is a place of great beauty and mystery, where the secrets of the universe are revealed. From the majestic temples of Tamil Nadu to the lush green hills of Kerala, this journey takes readers on a captivating exploration of India's mystical south.

The journey begins in the ancient city of Madurai, where the great temple of Meenakshi stands as a testament to the power of faith and devotion. Here, visitors can explore the intricately carved sculptures and marvel at the grandeur of the temple complex. From Madurai, the journey continues to the sacred groves of Kerala, where the ancient sages and mystics of India have sought refuge for centuries. Here, visitors can explore the lush green hills and experience the spiritual energy of the land.

The journey then takes travelers to the majestic temples of Tamil Nadu, where the secrets of the universe are revealed. From the grandeur of the Brihadeeswarar Temple to the intricate carvings of the Chidambaram Temple, visitors can explore the ancient architecture and marvel at the beauty of the temples.

Finally, the journey ends in the mystical city of Kanyakumari, where the sun rises and sets over the Indian Ocean. Here, visitors can experience the spiritual energy of the land and explore the ancient temples and monuments.

The Land of the Siddhas is a place of unparalleled beauty and intrigue, where the secrets of the cosmos are unveiled. Embarking on this journey, readers can discover the spiritual and cultural richness of India and gain a unique insight into its ancient traditions.

"India is the land of the yogi, the land of the mystic, and the land of the enlightened."

- Swami Vivekananda

ॐ

VIII

The Sacred Tirthas of India: Pilgrimage as a Path to Enlightenment

India is a land of spiritual and cultural richness, and its sacred tirthas are a testament to this. Tirthas are pilgrimage sites, and for centuries, they have been places of spiritual enlightenment and transformation. The practice of pilgrimage to these sites has been an integral part of Indian culture for millennia, and it is still a popular practice today.

The concept of pilgrimage is deeply rooted in the Indian spiritual tradition. It is believed that by visiting these sacred sites, one can gain spiritual insight and enlightenment.

Pilgrims often undertake arduous journeys to these sites, often walking for days or weeks to reach them. Along the way, they are often met with challenges and obstacles, which are seen as tests of their faith and commitment.

The most famous of India's tirthas are the four dhams, or abodes of the gods. These are Badrinath, Dwarka, Puri, and Rameshwaram. Each of these sites is associated with a particular deity, and pilgrims visit them to seek blessings and spiritual guidance. Other popular tirthas include the Ganges, the Yamuna, and the Narmada rivers, as well as the holy cities of Varanasi and Haridwar.

Pilgrimage to these sites is seen as a path to enlightenment. It is believed that by undertaking this journey, one can gain insight into the nature of the divine and the true nature of reality. Pilgrims often come away from these sites with a newfound sense of peace and understanding.

The practice of pilgrimage is not only a spiritual journey, but also a cultural one. Pilgrims often come away with a greater appreciation for the culture and traditions of India. They also gain a deeper understanding of the country's history and its spiritual heritage.

Pilgrimage to spiritual sites in India has been a practice for centuries and continues to be an important part of the country's cultural and spiritual heritage. These journeys are often seen as a way to purify the mind and body, and to deepen one's spiritual connection with the divine.

Pilgrimages can be physically and mentally challenging, and require a significant amount of devotion and discipline.

However, the rewards of the journey are believed to be immense, as pilgrims often come away with a newfound sense of peace, clarity, and purpose.

In addition to the spiritual benefits, pilgrimage also offers a unique cultural experience. Pilgrims have the opportunity to interact with local communities and to learn about the traditions and customs of the region. They may also have the chance to participate in traditional festivals and rituals, and to sample the local cuisine.

Pilgrimage is also a way for individuals to connect with their cultural heritage and to gain a deeper understanding of the country's spiritual legacy. India is home to some of the world's most revered spiritual sites, and the pilgrimage to these sites provides a glimpse into the rich history and spiritual traditions of the country.

Pilgrimage to spiritual sites in India is seen as a path to enlightenment and a means of deepening one's spiritual connection with the divine. It is a cultural and spiritual journey that provides pilgrims with a sense of peace and understanding, as well as a deeper appreciation for the culture and traditions of India.

"India is a land of mysticism and spirituality, a place where ancient traditions and beliefs still thrive."

ဆ

IX

The Great Saint of India: An overview of the Different spiritual leaders and Masters

India has been known for centuries as a land of spirituality, home to a rich and diverse culture steeped in religion and tradition. From ancient times to the present day, India has been a source of inspiration and guidance for millions of people in search of spiritual enlightenment. At the heart of this rich cultural heritage are the great saints and spiritual leaders of India, who have dedicated their lives to the pursuit of wisdom and the promotion of peace and harmony.

One of the earliest and most revered spiritual leaders in India was the Sage Vyasa, who is considered to be the author of the Vedas, the Hindu scriptures. Another notable spiritual master of ancient times was the Sage Patanjali, who wrote the Yoga Sutras, a seminal text on the science of yoga.

In the medieval period, India saw the rise of several great saints, including the Sufi saints Kabir and Rumi, and the Bhakti saints Mirabai, Chaitanya Mahaprabhu, and Ramananda. These saints advocated for a more direct and personal relationship with the divine, and their teachings and poems inspired countless devotees and followers.

In more recent times, India has produced a number of spiritual leaders and masters who have had a profound impact on the country and the world. One such figure was the great saint Sri Ramakrishna, who lived in the 19th century and taught the unity of all religions. His disciple, Swami Vivekananda, took this message of unity to the West and inspired many people with his teachings on yoga and spirituality.

Another important spiritual leader of recent times was Mahatma Gandhi, who inspired millions with his philosophy of nonviolence and his efforts to achieve independence for India. Another notable spiritual leader was Sri Aurobindo, who combined the pursuit of spiritual enlightenment with social and political activism.

In addition to these great saints and spiritual leaders, India has also produced many other accomplished masters, including Sri Nisargadatta Maharaj, Jiddu Krishnamurti,

Anandamayi Ma, and Sri Satya Sai Baba. These figures have left a lasting impact on the spiritual landscape of India and continue to inspire countless people around the world.

India is a land of great spiritual richness and diversity, with a long and proud tradition of great saints and spiritual leaders. From ancient times to the present day, these great figures have dedicated their lives to the pursuit of wisdom, peace, and harmony, and their teachings continue to inspire and guide people on the path of spiritual enlightenment.

"India is a kaleidoscope of culture, a place where the past and present come together in harmony."

༄

X

The Tribal Spirituality of India: Exploring the Hidden Traditions

India is a land of ancient traditions and spiritual practices, many of which are still alive today. Among these are the tribal spiritualities of India, which have been passed down through generations and remain deeply embedded in the culture. These spiritualities are often hidden from the outside world, but they are an integral part of the Indian experience.

The tribal spiritualities of India are rooted in the belief that the universe is composed of a variety of spiritual forces, and that these forces can be accessed through rituals and practices. These spiritualities are often associated with nature and the environment, and they are often seen as a way to connect with the divine.

The tribal spiritualities of India are often expressed through music, dance, and art. Music is used to invoke the spiritual forces, while dance is used to express the emotions associated with them. Art is used to depict the spiritual forces and to create a visual representation of them.

The tribal spiritualities of India are also expressed through the use of symbols and rituals. Symbols are used to represent the spiritual forces, while rituals are used to invoke them. These rituals often involve offerings, prayers, and chants.

The tribal spiritualities of India are also expressed through the use of sacred objects. These objects are often used in rituals and ceremonies, and they are believed to have special powers. These objects are often seen as a way to connect with the spiritual forces.

The tribal spiritualities of India are also expressed through the use of stories and myths. These stories and myths are often used to explain the spiritual forces and to provide guidance on how to interact with them.

The spiritual traditions of India are an integral part of the culture, deeply ingrained in the Indian psyche. They provide a means of connecting with the divine and expressing one's emotions in a meaningful way. These spiritualities are a source of strength and solace, allowing individuals to tap into a higher power and find peace in their lives.

The stories and myths that are central to tribal spiritualities in India are rich in symbolism and meaning, and often serve as allegories for the human experience. They often feature gods, goddesses, and other spiritual beings that embody various aspects of human nature and the natural world. Through these stories, individuals are able to explore their own emotions, experiences, and relationships with the spiritual forces that shape their lives.

The oral tradition of storytelling is an important part of tribal spiritualities in India, with tales being passed down from generation to generation. This tradition not only serves to preserve the cultural heritage of the tribes, but also allows for the evolution of the stories and the incorporation of new ideas and experiences.

In addition to storytelling, tribal spiritualities are also expressed through a variety of rituals and ceremonies. These rituals are often performed to mark important events or transitions in life, such as birth, death, and marriage, and serve to strengthen the individual's connection with the spiritual forces and the community.

Tribal spiritualities in India also play a significant role in the preservation of the natural world. They often include beliefs and practices that aim to maintain balance and harmony between humans and the environment. For example, many tribes have rituals that are performed to thank the spirits of the forest for their bounty and to ask for their protection.

The spiritual traditions of India's tribes are a rich and diverse expression of the human spirit, deeply rooted in the cultural heritage of the country. Through stories, rituals, and ceremonies, individuals are able to connect with the divine, explore their emotions, and find peace in their lives. These spiritualities serve as a source of strength and solace, and play a vital role in the preservation of the natural world and the cultural heritage of India.

"India is a land of beauty and wonder, a place of spiritual exploration and enlightenment."

ꕥ

XI

The Mystical Monasteries of India: A Cultural and Spiritual Exploration of the Himalayas

India is home to some of the most mystical monasteries in the world, nestled in the majestic Himalayas. These monasteries are a source of spiritual and cultural exploration, offering a unique insight into the ancient traditions of India.

The Himalayas are a vast mountain range that stretches across India, Nepal, Bhutan, and Tibet. These mountains are home to some of the most sacred sites in India, including the monasteries of Ladakh, Sikkim, and Arunachal Pradesh. These monasteries are a testament to the ancient spiritual and cultural traditions of India, and offer a unique opportunity to explore the rich history of the region.

The monasteries of Ladakh are some of the most renowned in India. These monasteries are home to a variety of Buddhist sects, and offer a unique insight into the spiritual practices of the region. The monasteries of Sikkim are also renowned for their spiritual practices, and are home to a variety of Hindu and Buddhist sects. The monasteries of Arunachal Pradesh are home to a variety of tribal cultures, and offer a unique insight into the traditional customs of the region.

The monasteries of the Himalayas are a source of spiritual and cultural exploration, offering visitors a unique opportunity to explore the ancient traditions of India. From the sacred sites of Ladakh to the tribal cultures of Arunachal Pradesh, the monasteries of the Himalayas provide a unique insight into the spiritual and cultural heritage of India.

Visitors to the monasteries of the Himalayas can expect to experience a plethora of spiritual and cultural activities. From meditative prayer to traditional ceremonies and rituals, the monasteries of the Himalayas offer a one-of-a-kind opportunity to delve into the ancient traditions of India. Additionally, visitors can anticipate a variety of cultural activities, such as traditional music and dance, as well as the chance to explore the majestic beauty of the Himalayas.

The monasteries of the Himalayas are not just places of worship and devotion, but also centers of learning and cultural preservation. Visitors can attend teachings and lectures on Buddhist philosophy and meditation, and learn about the rich history and customs of the local communities. They can also participate in workshops on traditional arts and crafts, such as thangka painting and sculpting, and gain a deeper appreciation for the rich cultural heritage of the region.

One of the highlights of visiting the monasteries of the Himalayas is the chance to attend traditional religious ceremonies and rituals. These ceremonies, often accompanied by music and dance, offer a glimpse into the spiritual practices of the local communities and provide a sense of the deep reverence and devotion that is so central to the cultural fabric of the region.

The beauty of the Himalayas is also a major draw for visitors, and many monasteries offer opportunities to explore the surrounding wilderness through guided hikes and trekking expeditions. These adventures provide a unique opportunity to experience the natural beauty of the region, and to reflect on the spiritual significance of the mountains and the ancient traditions that have been practiced there for centuries.

For those seeking a more immersive experience, many monasteries also offer residential programs, where visitors can live and study in the community for an extended period of time. These programs provide a deeper understanding of the spiritual and cultural practices of the region, and offer a unique opportunity for personal growth and self-discovery.

The monasteries of the Himalayas offer a rich and diverse array of spiritual and cultural experiences for visitors. Whether you are seeking an introduction to ancient spiritual traditions, or a deeper immersion into the cultural heritage of the region, the monasteries of the Himalayas are a must-visit destination for those seeking a deeper understanding of the spiritual and cultural heritage of India.

Some More Quotes on India

"India is a place of ancient wisdom, a land of spiritual discovery and transformation."

"India is a land of mystery and enchantment, a place of spiritual awakening and exploration."

"India is a land of vibrant colors and rich culture, a place of spiritual growth and exploration."

"India is a place of spiritual exploration and enlightenment, a land of ancient wisdom and traditions."

"India is a land of sacred rituals and traditions, a place of spiritual growth and exploration."

"India is a place of spiritual awakening and exploration, a land of beauty and wonder."

"India is a land of ancient traditions and beliefs, a place of spiritual discovery and transformation."

"India is a place of spiritual growth and exploration, a land of vibrant colors and rich culture."

"India is a land of mysticism and enchantment, a place of spiritual awakening and exploration."

"India is a place of spiritual exploration and enlightenment, a land of sacred rituals and traditions."

"India is a land of ancient wisdom and traditions, a place of beauty and wonder."

"India is a kaleidoscope of culture, a place of spiritual growth and exploration."

༄

Other Books Of The Author

1. The Moments When I Met God
2. Kashiyile Theertha Pathangal
3. GURU GYAN VANI
4. Abhiprerak Gita
5. ASSI SE JAIN GHAT TAK
6. Hopelessness of Arjuna
7. The Soul and It's True Nature
8. Sense of Action (Karma)
9. Action through Wisdom
10. Action through Wisdom
11. THEORY AND PRACTICAL OF EVERY ACTION
12. LOGICAL UNDERSTANDING OF THE SUPREME
13. THE IMPERISHABLE SUPREME
14. Yatra Nishadraj se Hanuman Ghat Tak
15. Yatra Karnatak Ghat se Raja Ghat Tak
16. Yatra Pandey Ghat se Prayagraj Ghat Tak
17. Yatra Ranjendra Prasad Ghat se Dattatreya Ghat Tak
18. YaatraSindhiya Ghat se Gwaliar Ghat Tak
19. Yatra Mangala Gauri Ghat se Hanuman Gadhi Ghat Tak
20. Yatra Gaay Ghat Se Nishad Ghat Tak
21. MAA GANGA, GHATEN EVM UTSAV
22. Ganga Arti Dev Deepavali evam Any Utsav
23. Potentials of Digitalized India
24. VEDIC CONSCIOUSNESS
25. A Brief Introduction to Vedic Science
26. Kashi ke Barah Jyotirling
27. IMPACT OF MOTIVATION
28. Let's have a Milky Way Journey
29. Color Therapy in a Nutshell

30. Rigveda in a Nutshell
31. Yajurveda in a Nutshell
32. Samveda in a Nutshell
33. Atharva Veda in a Nutshell
34. Ayushman Bhava - Ayurveda
35. Srimad Bhagavad Gita and Upanishad Connection
36. Srimad Bhagavad Gita - an attempt to summarize each chapter.
37. Facts and Impact of Nakshatra
38. Astro Gems - NAVARATNA
39. Ekadashi - A Concise Overview
40. A Concise View of Hanuman Chalisa
41. Inspirational Gita
42. Nakshatraranyam
43. Summary of 18 Mahapuranas
44. Synopsis of 18 Upa Puranas
45. Rigvediya Upanishads
46. Shukla Yajurvediya Upanishads
47. Krishna Yajurvediya Upanishads
48. Samavediya Upanishads
49. Atharvavediya Upanishads
50. The Seven Great Sages
51. From Rocket Scientist to President Dr. APJ Abdul Kalam
52. The Visionary's Voice - Quotes of Dr. APJ Abdul Kalam
53. The Wisdom of Swami Vivekananda: Insights and Inspiration from a Legendary Spiritual Teacher
54. Ayurvedic Remedies from the Garden
55. Sages and Seers
56. Rising Strong – Motivational Stories of Women
57. Beyond Flames -Mystery stories of Funeral Ghat Manikarnika
58. The Origins of Tulsi: A Look at the Mythological Roots of the Plant"

59. The Holistic Cow: A Look at the Physical, Spiritual, and Cultural Importance of Cows in India
60. Arts of Healing
61. Exploring the Divine
62. Understanding Five Elements
63. The Etymology of Ram
64. Symbols of India
65. Voice of Change (About Speeches of Great Men)
66. She Speaks (About Speeches of Great Women)
67. Patriotism on Celluloid – Brief About Patriotic Films
68. The Music of Motivation: A Brief Guide to Inspirational Film Songs
69. **Unlocking the Secrets of the Dashopanishads**
70. A Cultural Mosaic
71. Ancient Traditions, Modern Minds
72. Ecos of Ancient Wisdom
73. Beneath the Surface
74. From Temples to Ashrams
75. Sages of the Subcontinent
76. The Art of Healling (Ayurveda, Yoga & Naturopathy)
77. Indian Kitchen
78. The Festivals of India
79. The Indian Epics Retold
80. The Power of Mantras
81. The Indian River Ganges
82. The Indian Architecture
83. Rites of Passage
84. The Indian Silk Road
85. The Indian Literature
86. The Indian Villages
87. The Indian Folks & Crafts
88. The Way of Buddha
89. The Ramayan of Tulsidas

90. Astrological Remedies
91. The Secret Power of Motivation
92. Secret of Developing your Inner Strength
93. The Secret Path to Motivation
94. The Art and Secret of Positive Thinking
95. The Secrets of Practicing Ethical Living
96. Indian Art and Painting
97. The Indian Herbalism
98. Bharatanatyam to Kathak
99. Exploring India's Astrological Remedies
100. The Indian Festival of Flowers
101. Indian Handicrafts
102. The Splashes of Joy – India's Colour Festival
103. The Indian Science of Astrology
104. The Indian Mythology
105. Path to Enlightenment
106. The Indian Spirituality for Children
107. Aromas of India
108. The Secrets of Healthy Relationships
109. Ancestral Ties
110. The Indian Street Food
111. Discovering America
112. The Indian Textile
113. Listening to Motivational Speeches
114. Taste of India
115. A Cultural Journey through Indian Nuptials
116. Motivational Quote for Change
117. Secret Strategies for Making Money
118. Secrets to Cultivate a Positive Mindset
119. A Tapestry of Cultures: Exploring India from Kashmir to Kanyakumari
120. Achieving Your Dreams with Resilience: Secret Strategies for Overcoming Obstacles

121. Innovative Startups - 25 Startup Ideas to Spark Your Business Creativity
122. Export Management: Strategies for Global Success
123. Exporting from India - A Step by Step Guide
124. Finance Fundamentals: Mastering Financial Management for Business Success
125. Global Growth Strategies for International Business Development
126. Marketing Mastery: Unlocking the Secrets of Modern Marketing
127. Operations Mastery: Managing the Flow of Value in Business
128. Strategic Business Management: Navigating the Modern Business Landscape
129. Human Resource Management Strategies for Building and Managing a High Performance Team
130. The Indian Landscapes and Nature: An Exploration Of India's Natural Beauty And Diversity
131. The Indian Street Performances: A Cultural Exploration of India's Street Performances
132. Affirming Your Self-Worth: Strategies for Achieving Emotional Wellbeing
133. Cultivating Self-Discipline: Secrets Methods for Achieving Your Goals
134. Embracing Change: Strategies for Adapting to Life's Challenges
135. Embracing Your Uniqueness: Secret Strategies for Living an Authentic Life
136. Finding Motivation in Despondency: Coping with Difficult Times
137. Embracing Change
138. Learning to Love Yourself
139. Managing Time for Yourself

140. Unlock the keys to Self-Motivation
141. Secret to Boost Confidence
142. Unlocking your Potential: A Path to Inner-strength & Success
143. Secrets to Develop Authentic Relationship
144. Secrets to Build a Successful Career
145. Secrets to Live with Gratitude
146. Secrets to Create a Life of Abundance
147. Secrets to Cultivate Self-Awareness
148. The Power of Helping Hands
149. Finding Your Passion
150. The Indian Mythical Creatures
151. The Indian Women Saints
152. The Wisdom of the Saints
153. "The Indian Royalty: A Cultural and Historical Exploration of India's Maharajas and their kingdom"
154. The Mystic Land: A Cultural and Spiritual Exploration of India"

Contact

DR. JAGADEESH PILLAI

MBA & PhD in Vedic Science

Four Times Guinness World Record Holder

Winner of Mahatma Gandhi Vishwa Shanti Puraskar and Global Peace Ambassador

Gemology, Astro & Vastu Consultant - Spiritual Counselor

Consultant for designing World Record Ideas

Efficient Tarot Card Reader

9839093003

myrichindia@gmail.com

drjagadeeshpillai@facebook

drjagadeeshpillai@instagram
jagadeeshpillai@youtube

www. JAGADEESHPILLAI.com

|| LOKAHA SAMASTHAHA SUKHINO BHAVANTU ||

Printed by Libri Plureos GmbH in Hamburg, Germany